Kaye Dennan

DOLPHIN FAVORITES

Coloring And Numbers Book

For Children Aged 5-8

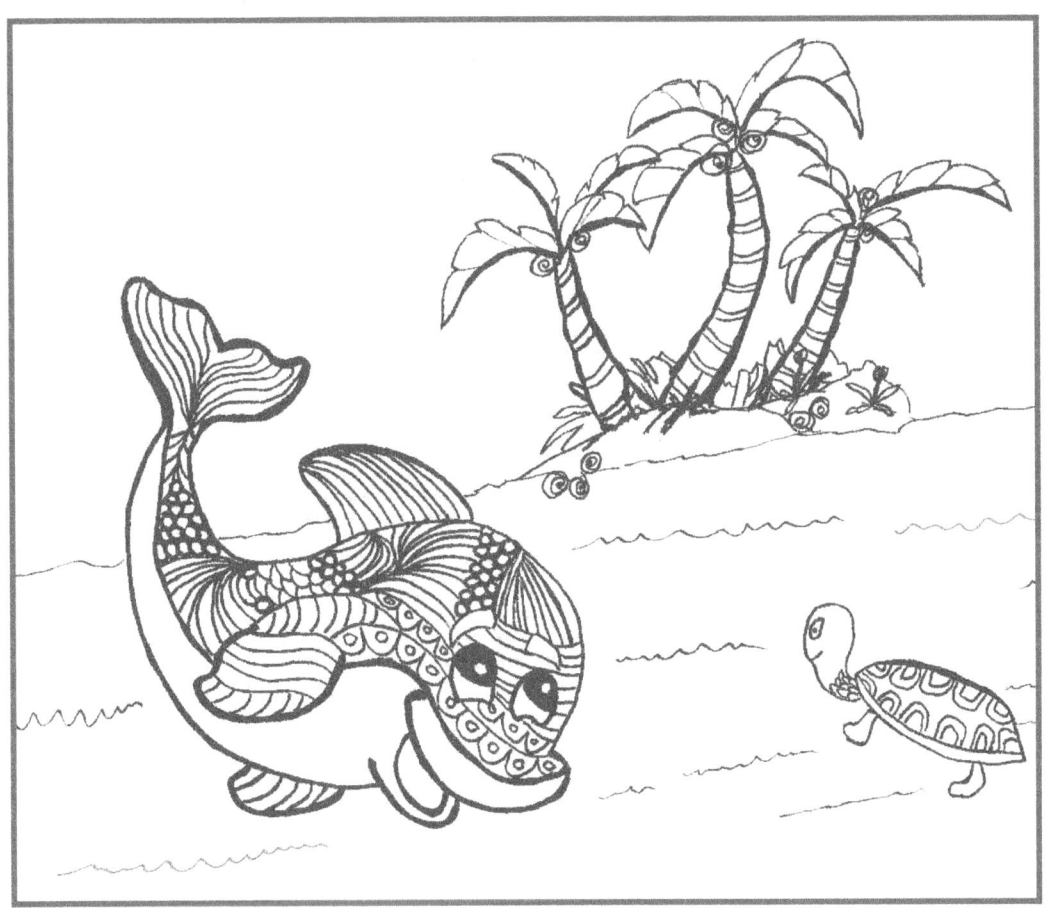

By: Kaye Dennan
ISBN-13: 978-1727226829

Kaye Dennan

A note from the Author/Illustrator

Included in this book are color images to help with your coloring experience. The images you have to color are just a guide, feel free to add or detract from the picture as you so wish. Creating your very own style can be fun and very satisfying.

Some images have been produced in grayscale so that you can easily color over the lines rather than have black outlines in your picture.

Every second page has been left blank so that you do not ruin one of your colored designs with color bleeding through the back of the page.

If you are using pencils then I would suggest you slide a piece of thin cardboard or thick paper under the page you are coloring just to prevent any pressure marks on the following page.

Please feel free to share your picture on my pages:

Facebook   https://www.facebook.com/InfoEbooksOnline/

Pinterest   https://www.pinterest.com/KayeDennan/

PUBLISHERS NOTES
Disclaimer

All Rights Reserved. No part of this publication may be reproduced in any form or by any means, including scanning, photocopying, or otherwise without prior written permission of the copyright holder.

Copyright © 2018 Kaye Dennan

Paperback Edition

Manufactured in the United States of America

ABOUT DOLPHINS

Dolphins are a very popular mammal and even more so today because we can now travel to places where you can swim with dolphins and this has increased their popularity no end.

Dolphins range in size from the 1.7 metres (5.6 ft) long and 50 kilograms (110 lb) of Maui's dolphin to the 9.5 metres (31 ft) and 10 metric tons (11 short tons) killer whale. In several species the males are larger than females.

They have streamlined bodies and two limbs that are modified into flippers. Some dolphins can travel at 55.5 kilometres per hour (34.5 mph) and travel long distances.

Dolphins use their conical shaped teeth to capture fast moving prey and largely feed on squid and fish. They have well-developed hearing – their hearing is adapted for both air and water. Some species are well adapted for diving to great depths and have a layer of fat, or blubber, under the skin to keep warm in the cold water.

Most species of dolphin prefer the warmer waters of the tropical zones and it is quite common to see them near beaches and swimming alongside yachts and other boats. They will often accompany boats for quite long distances, swimming near the bow of the boat and up in front of it.

Male dolphins typically mate with multiple females every year, but females only mate every two to three years. Calves are typically born in the spring and summer months and females bear all the responsibility for raising them. Mothers often nurse their young for a relatively long period of time.

Dolphins produce a variety of vocalizations, usually in the form of clicks and whistles. These calling sounds can actually be quite loud and easy to hear if they are travelling alongside you when boating.

We tend to be very familiar with the bottlenose dolphin because that is the species that is most often kept in captivity and trained to perform tricks.

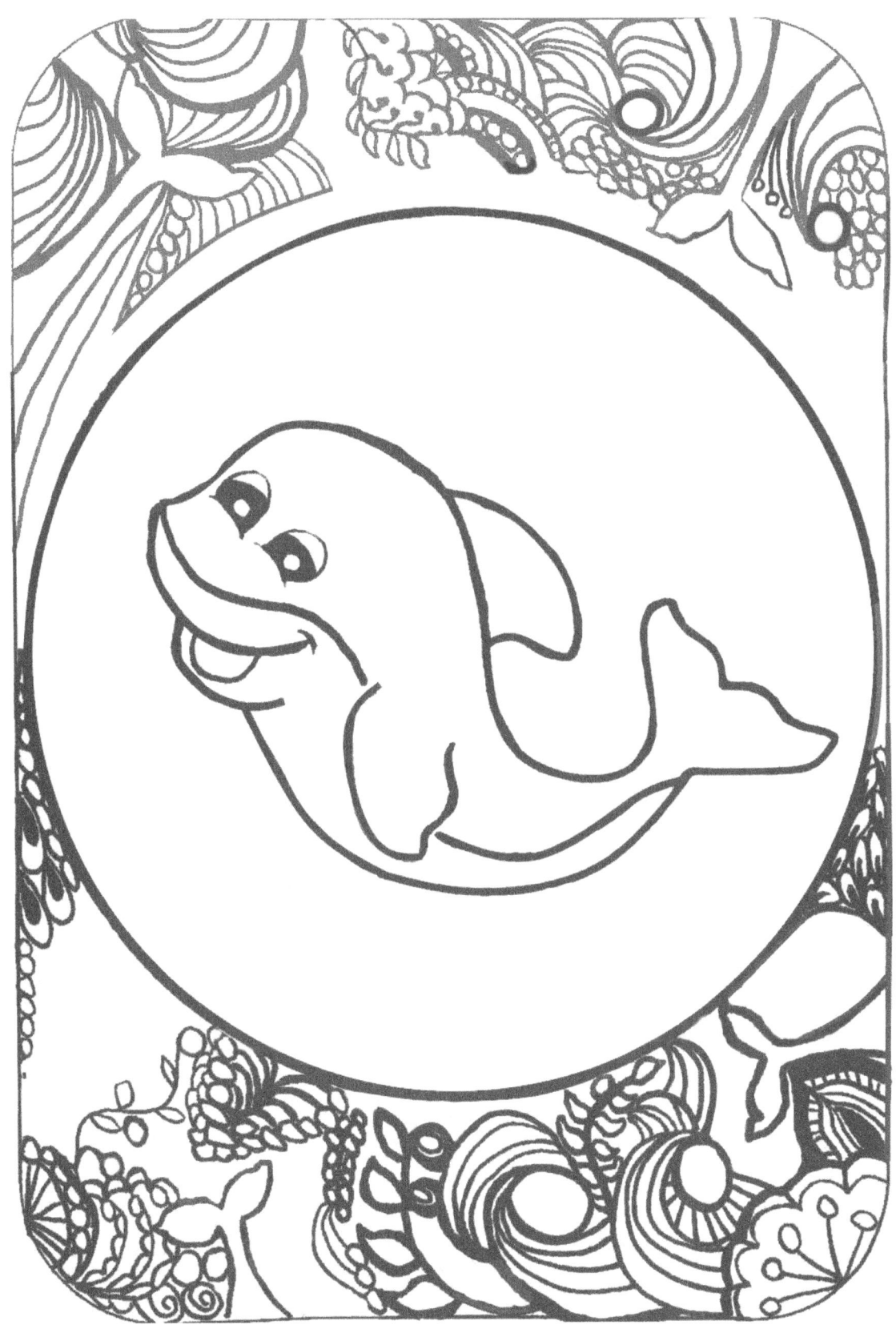

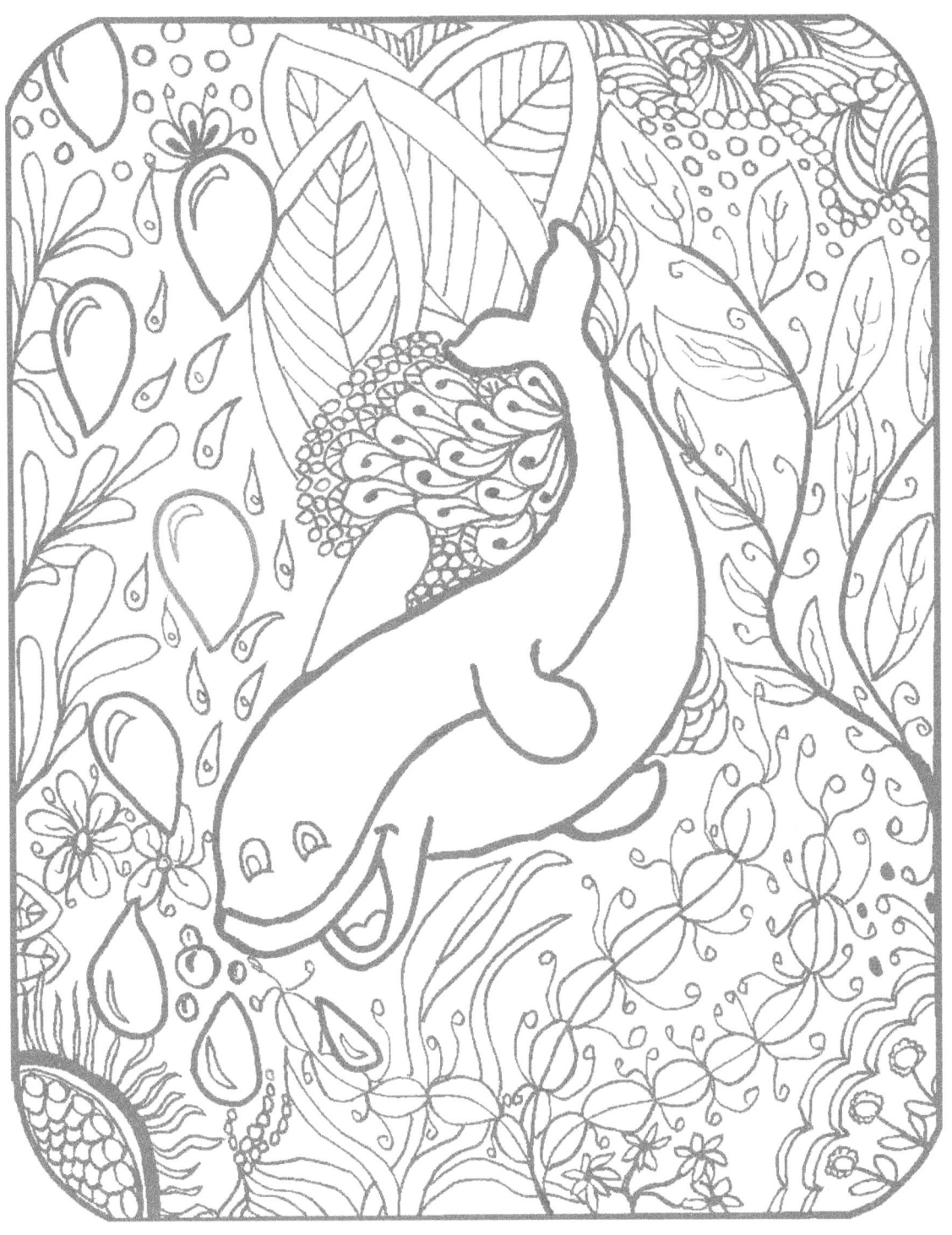

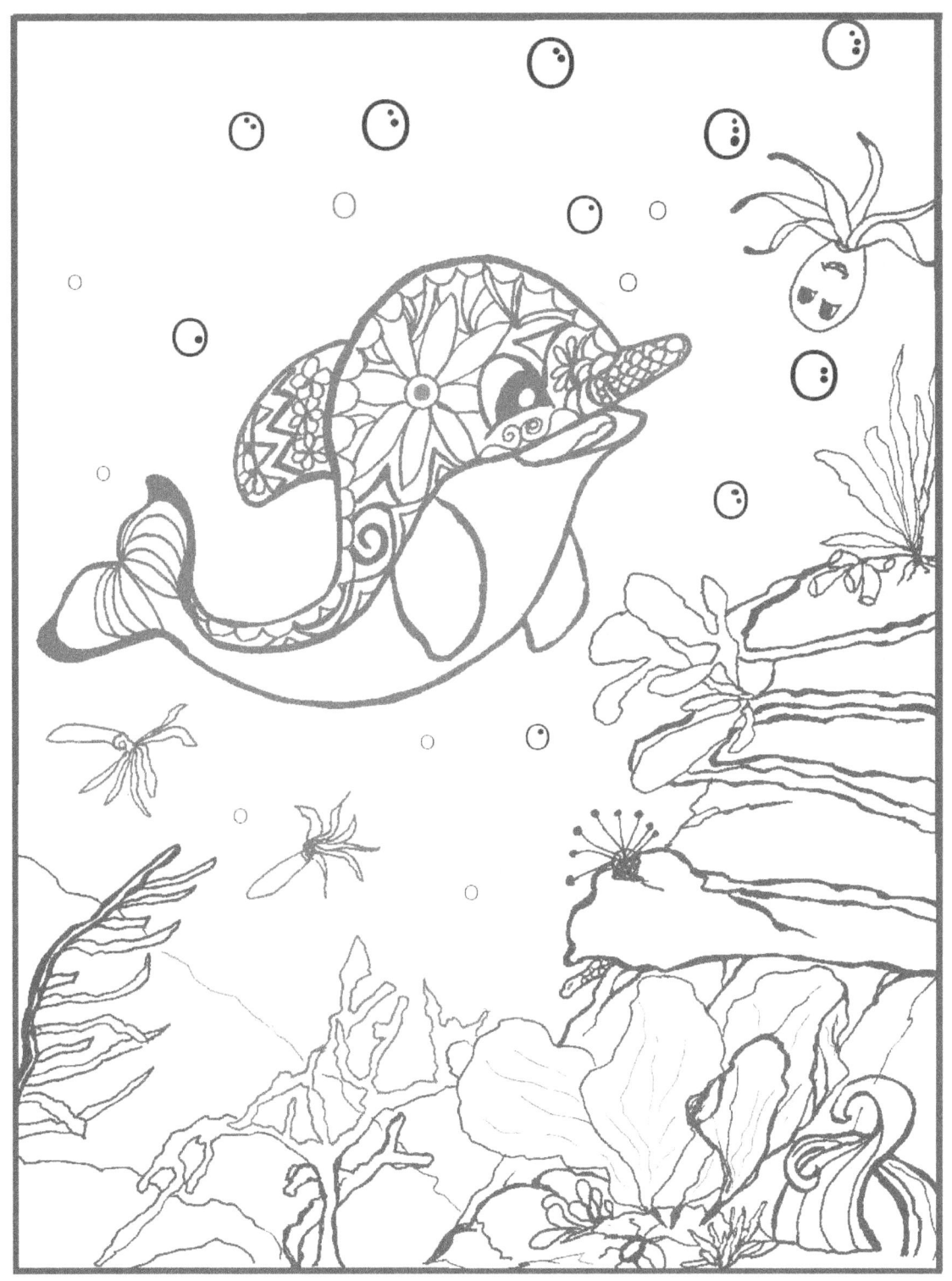

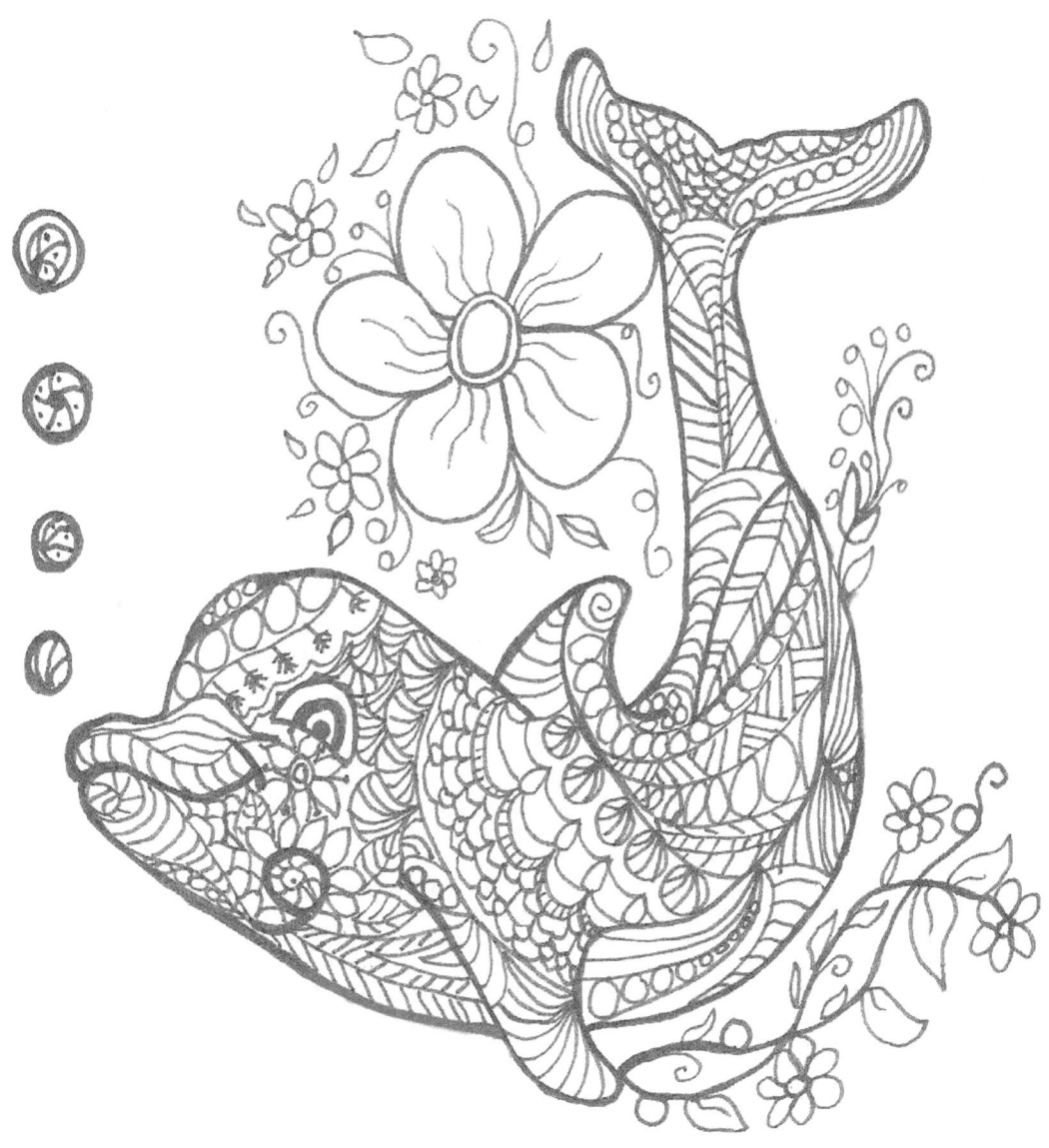

Magic Number 6

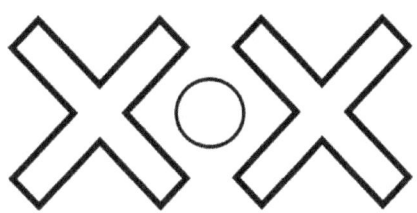

1. Write it   _____

2. Draw it   _____

3. Add 5   _____

4. Subtract 3   _____

5. Add 4   _____

6. Subtract 2   _____

7. Next 3 numbers _____ _____ _____

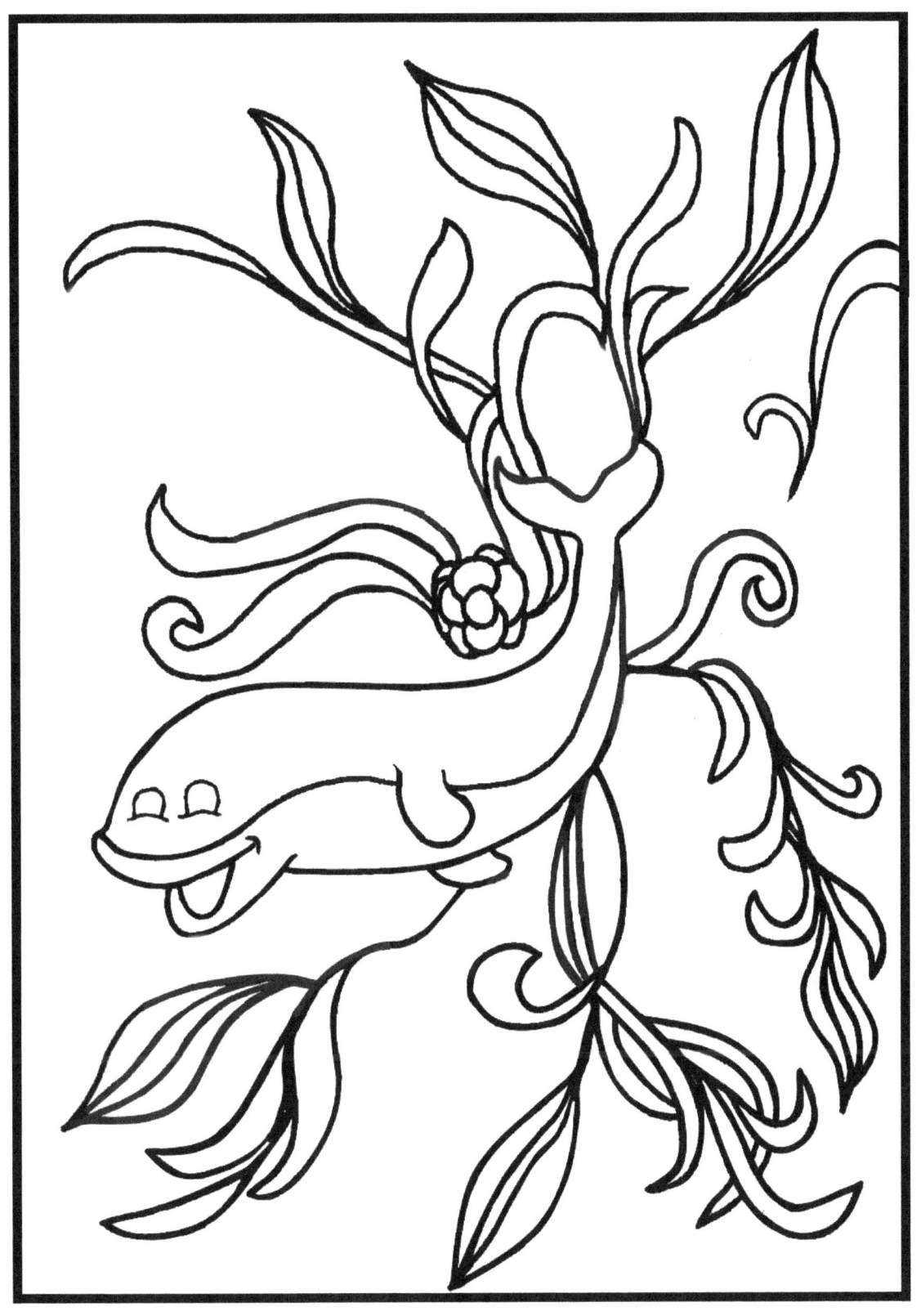

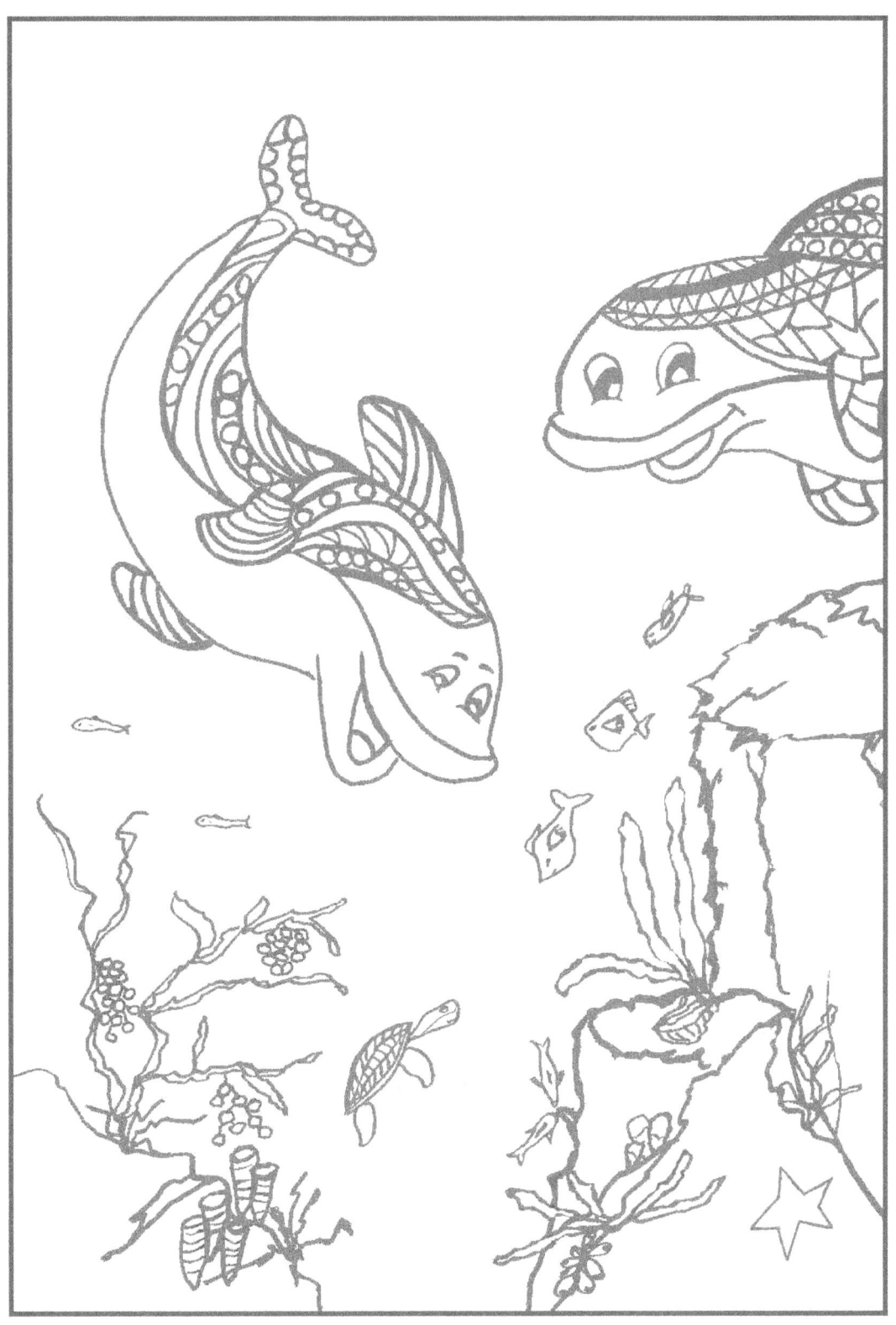

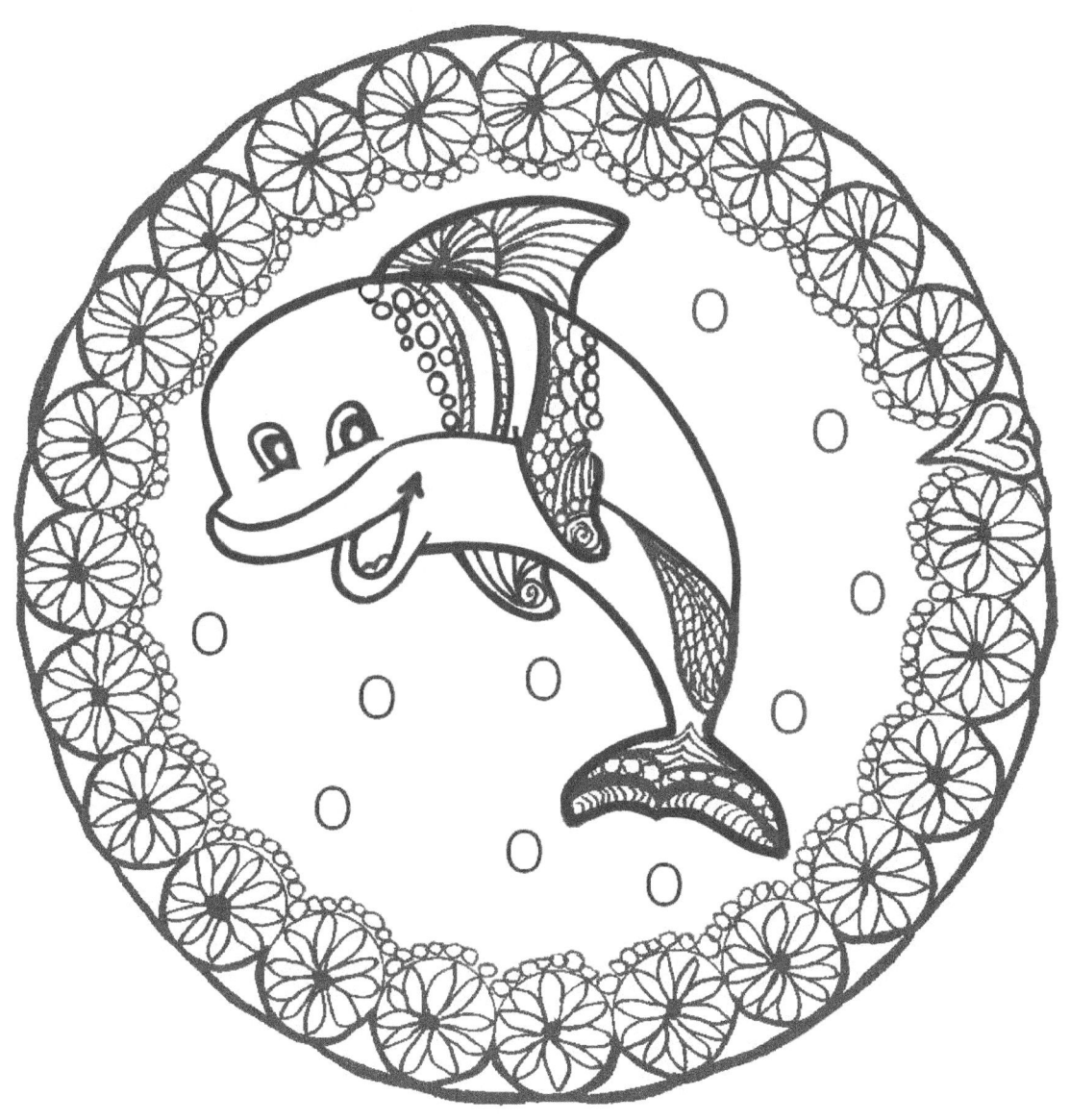

Magic Number   9

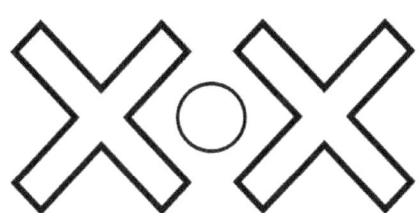

1. Write it   _____

2. Draw it   _____

3. Add 4   _____

4. Subtract 5   _____

5. Add 6   _____

6. Subtract 6   _____

7. Next 3 numbers _____   _____   _____

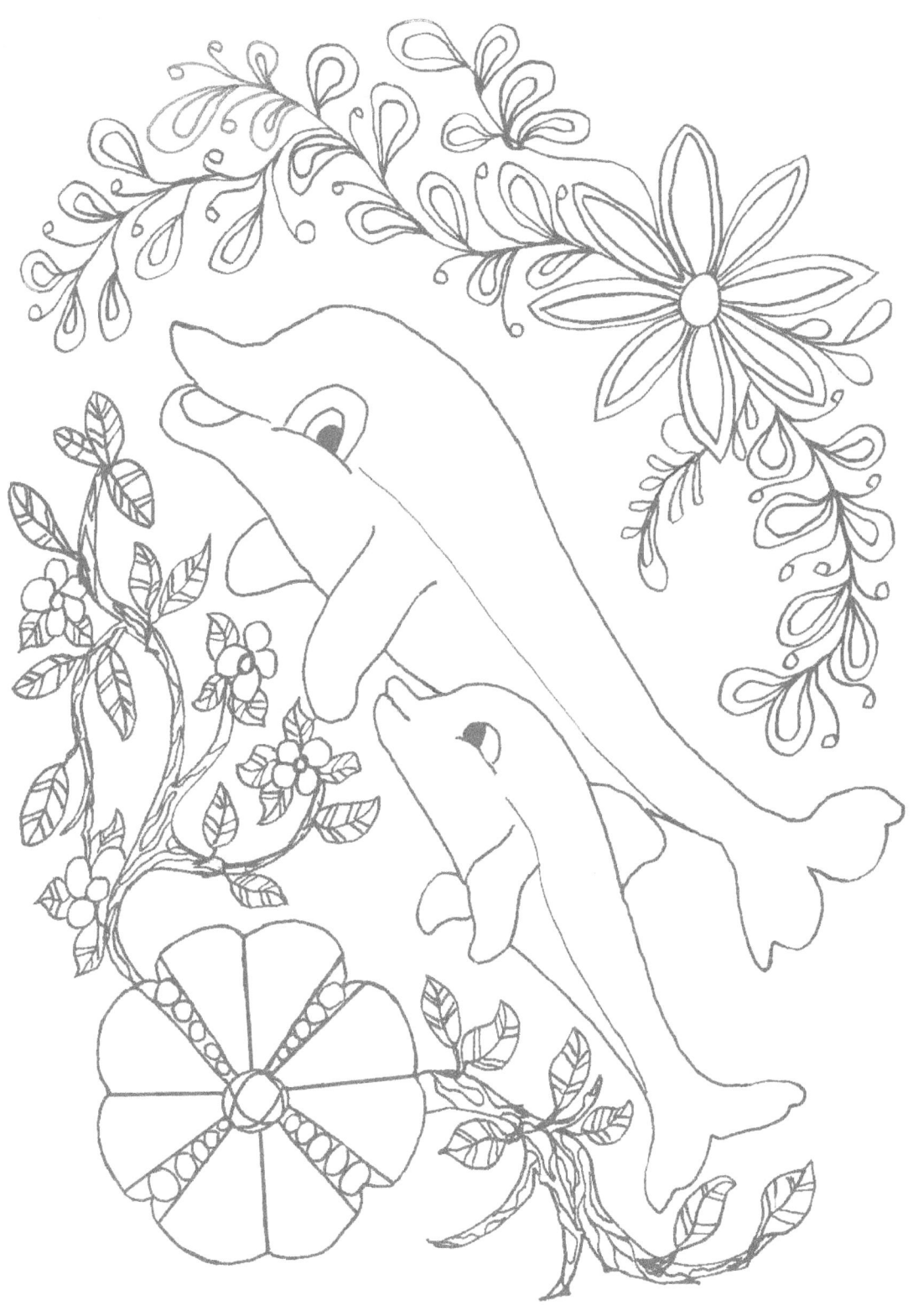

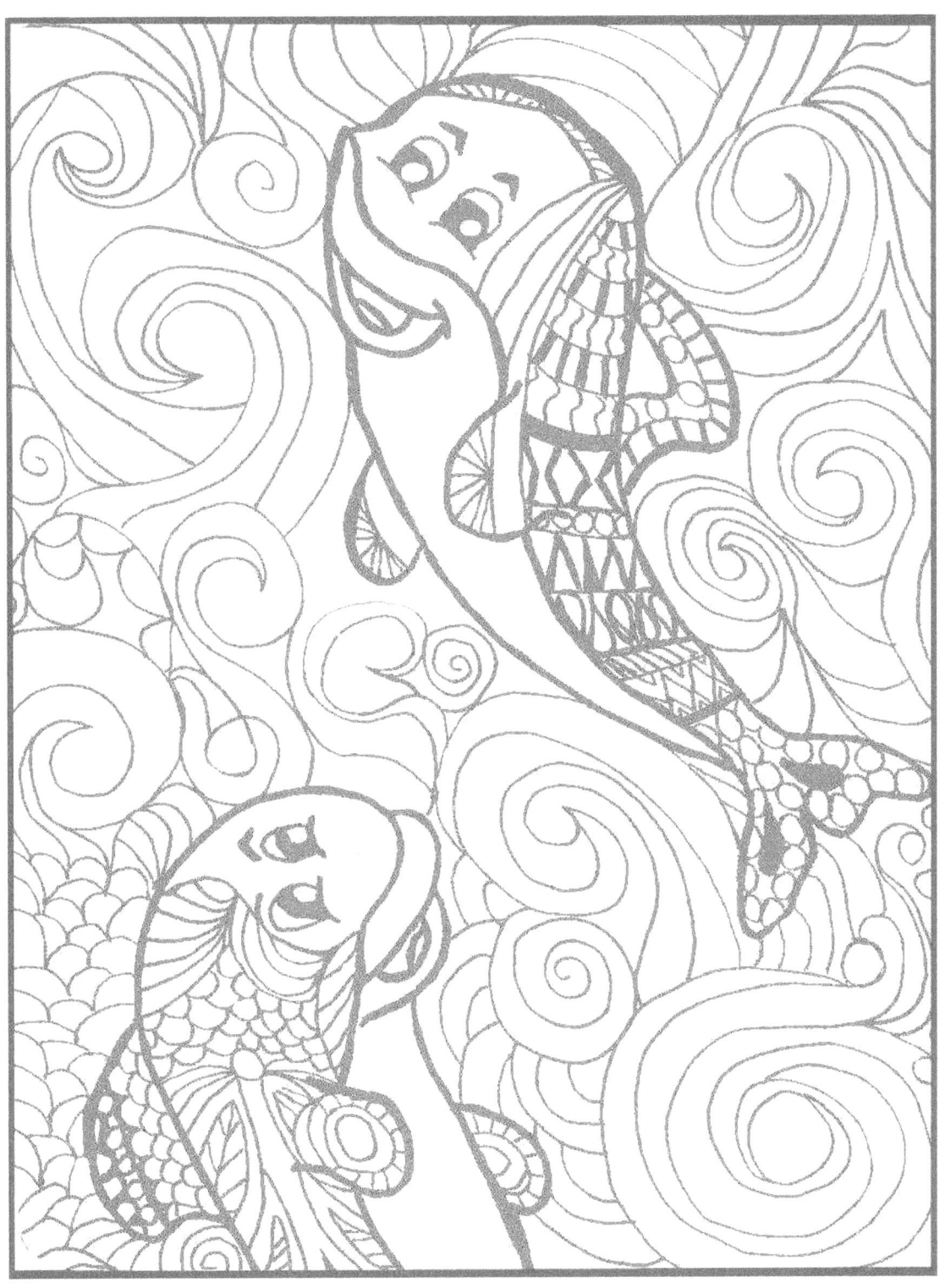

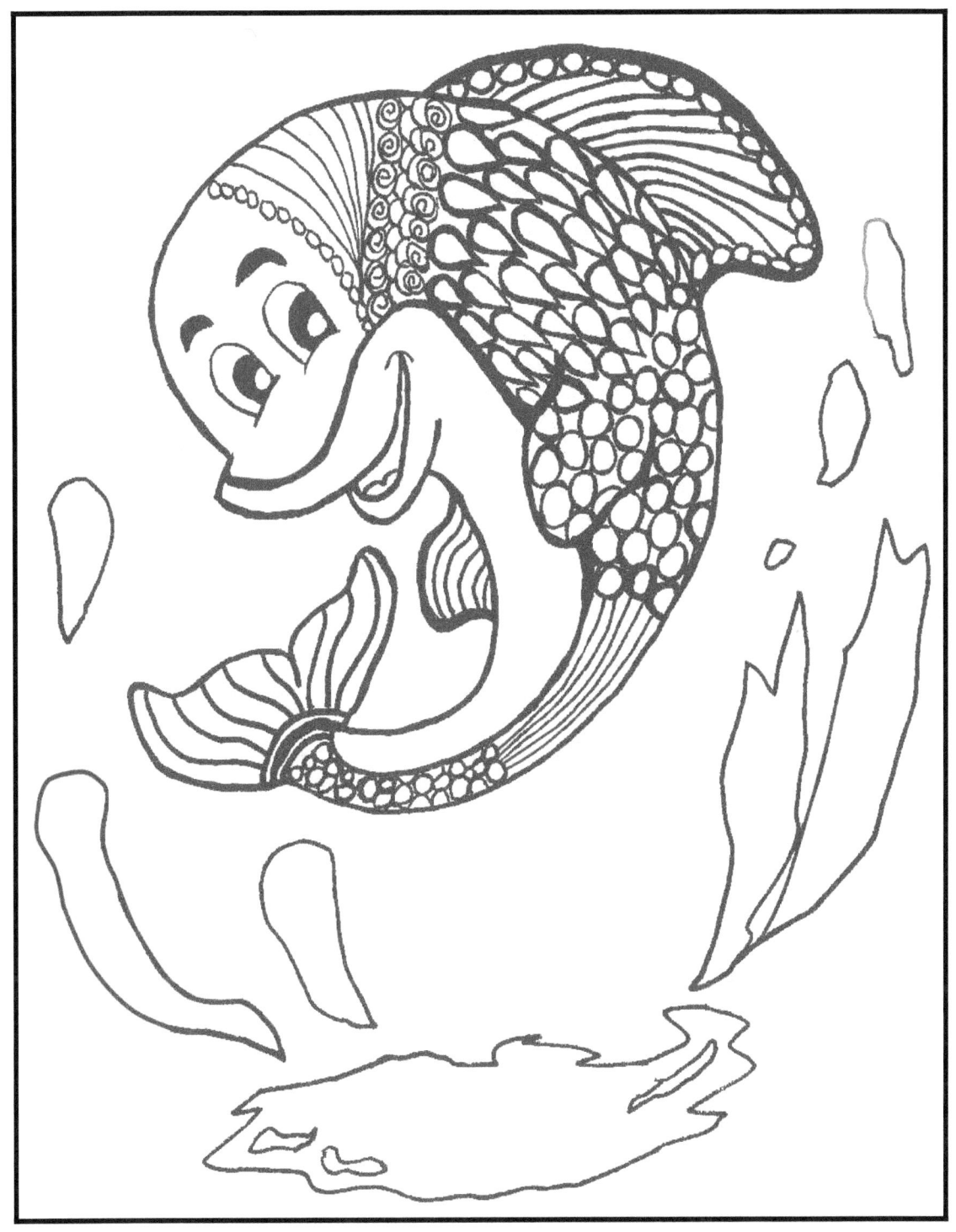

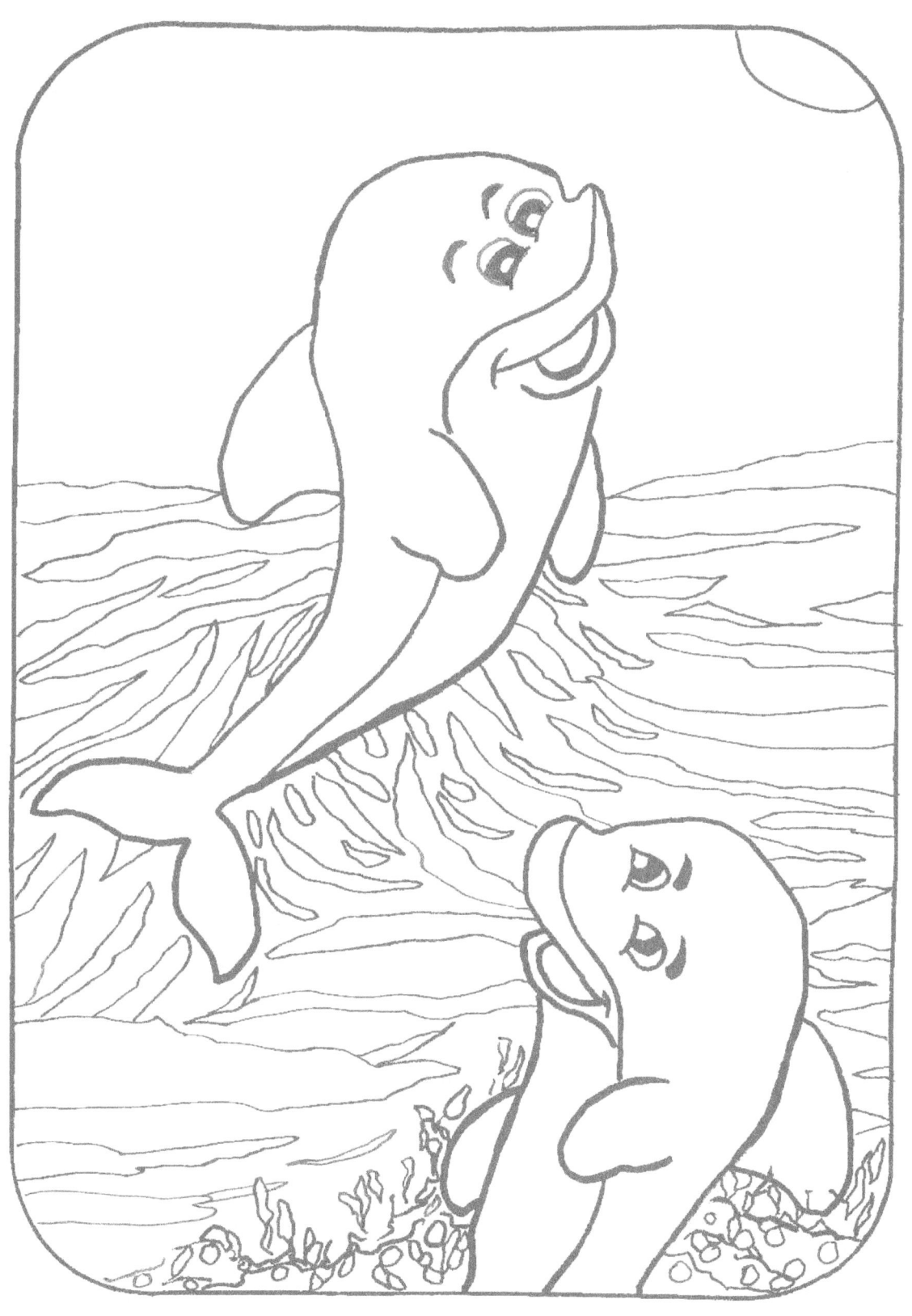

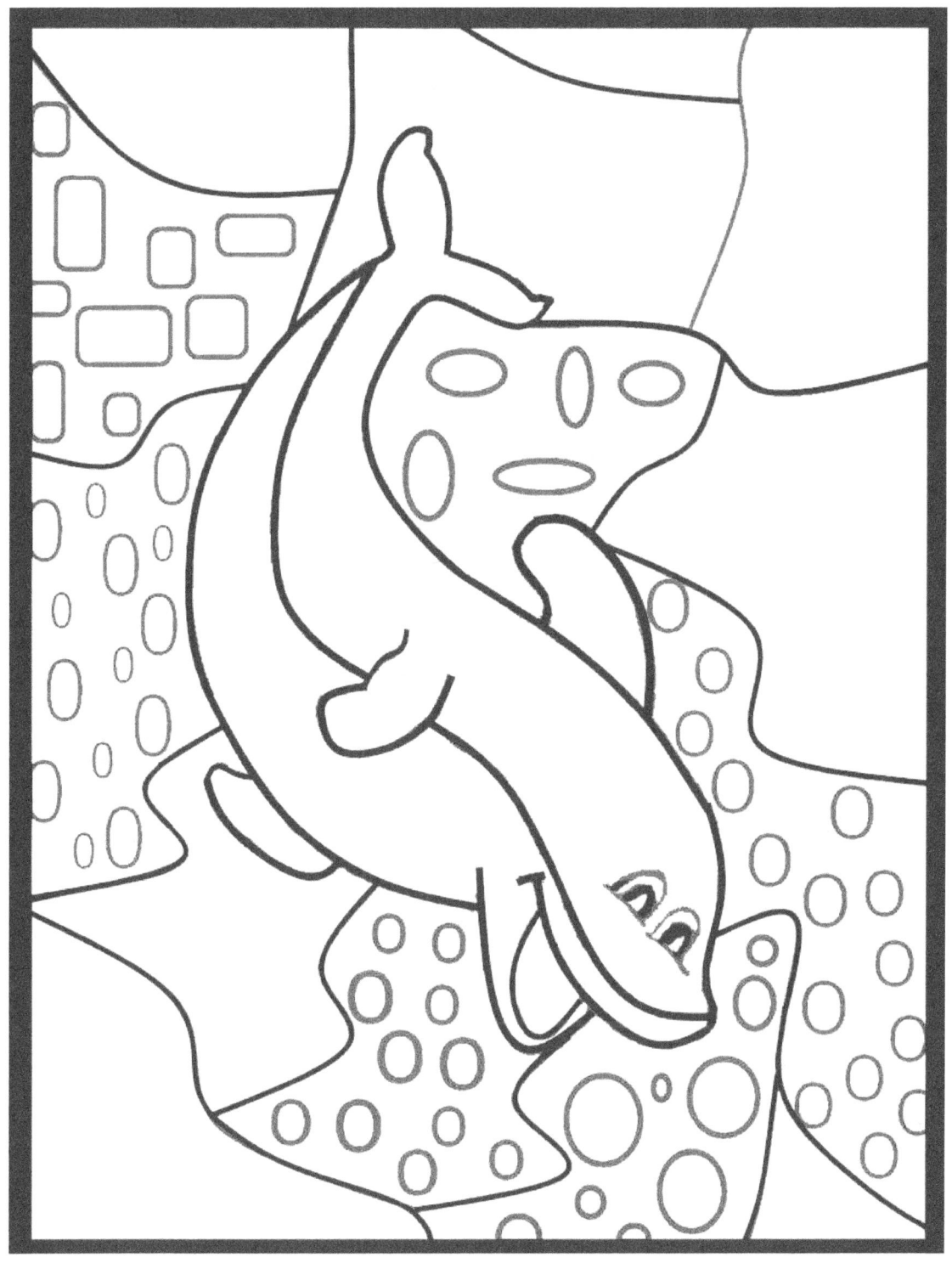

Magic Number 7

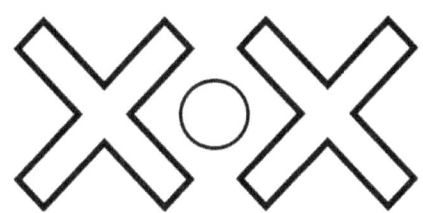

1. Write it   _____

2. Draw it   _____

3. Add 3   _____

4. Subtract 4   _____

5. Add 2   _____

6. Subtract 3   _____

7. Next 3 numbers ____ ____ ____

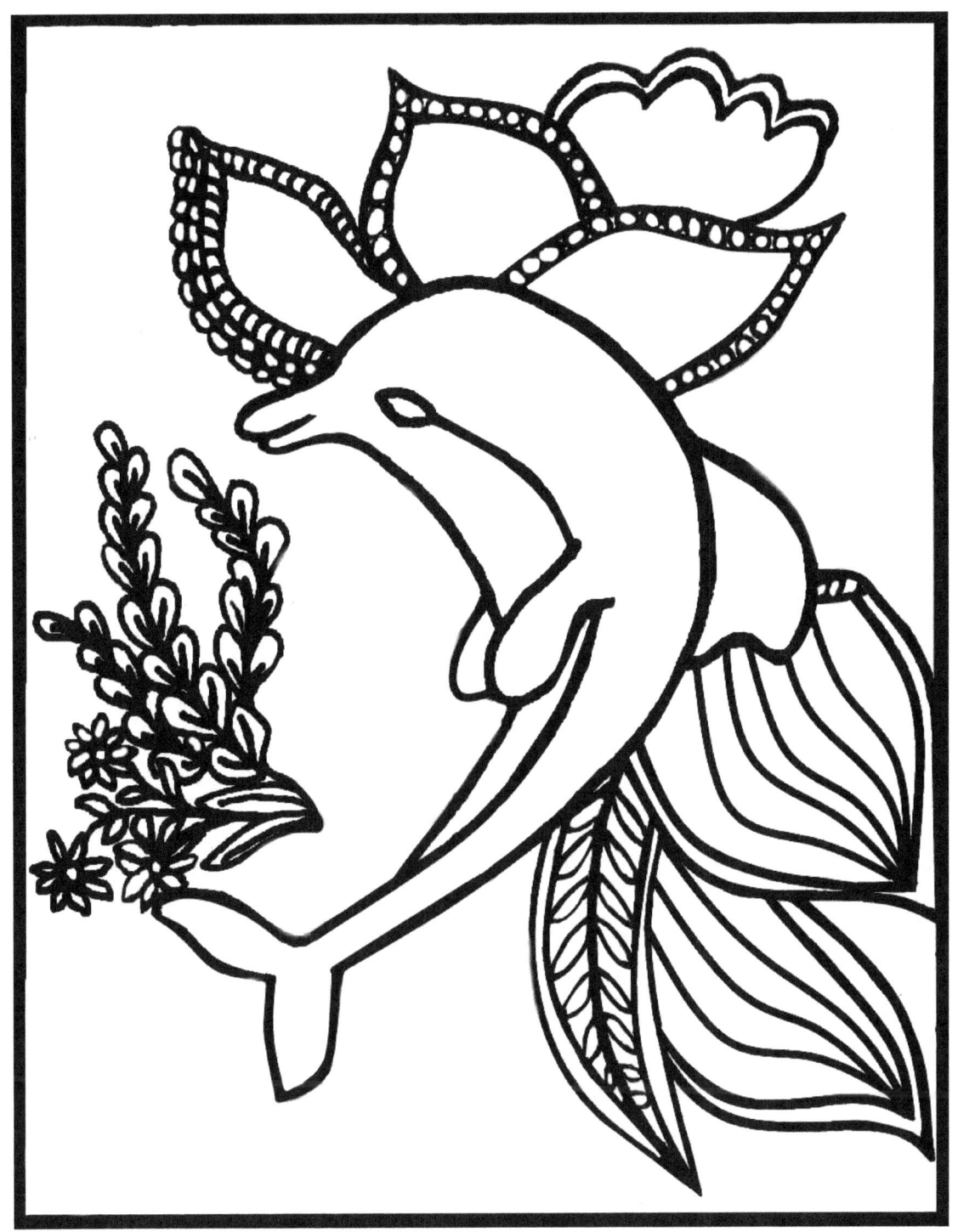

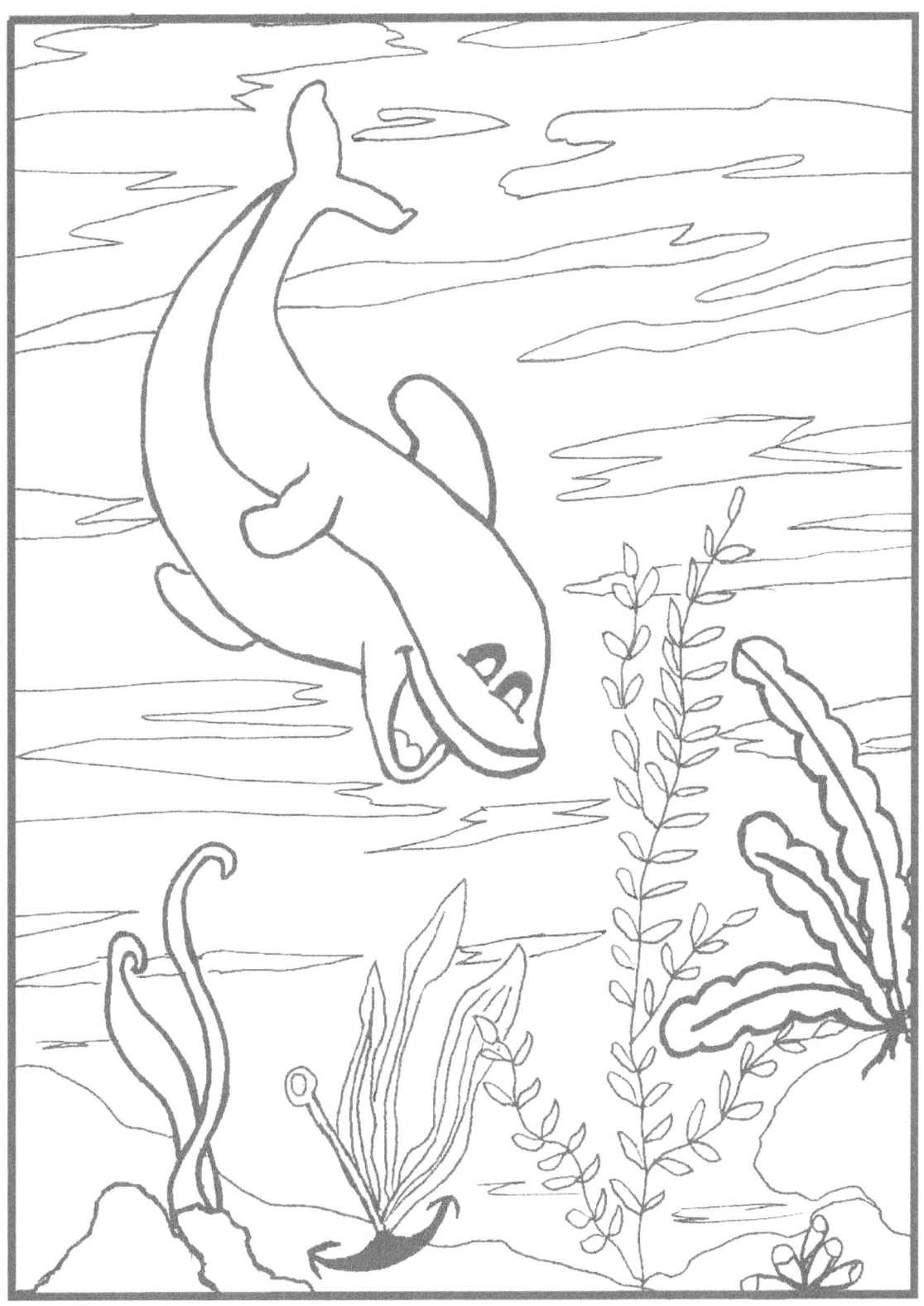

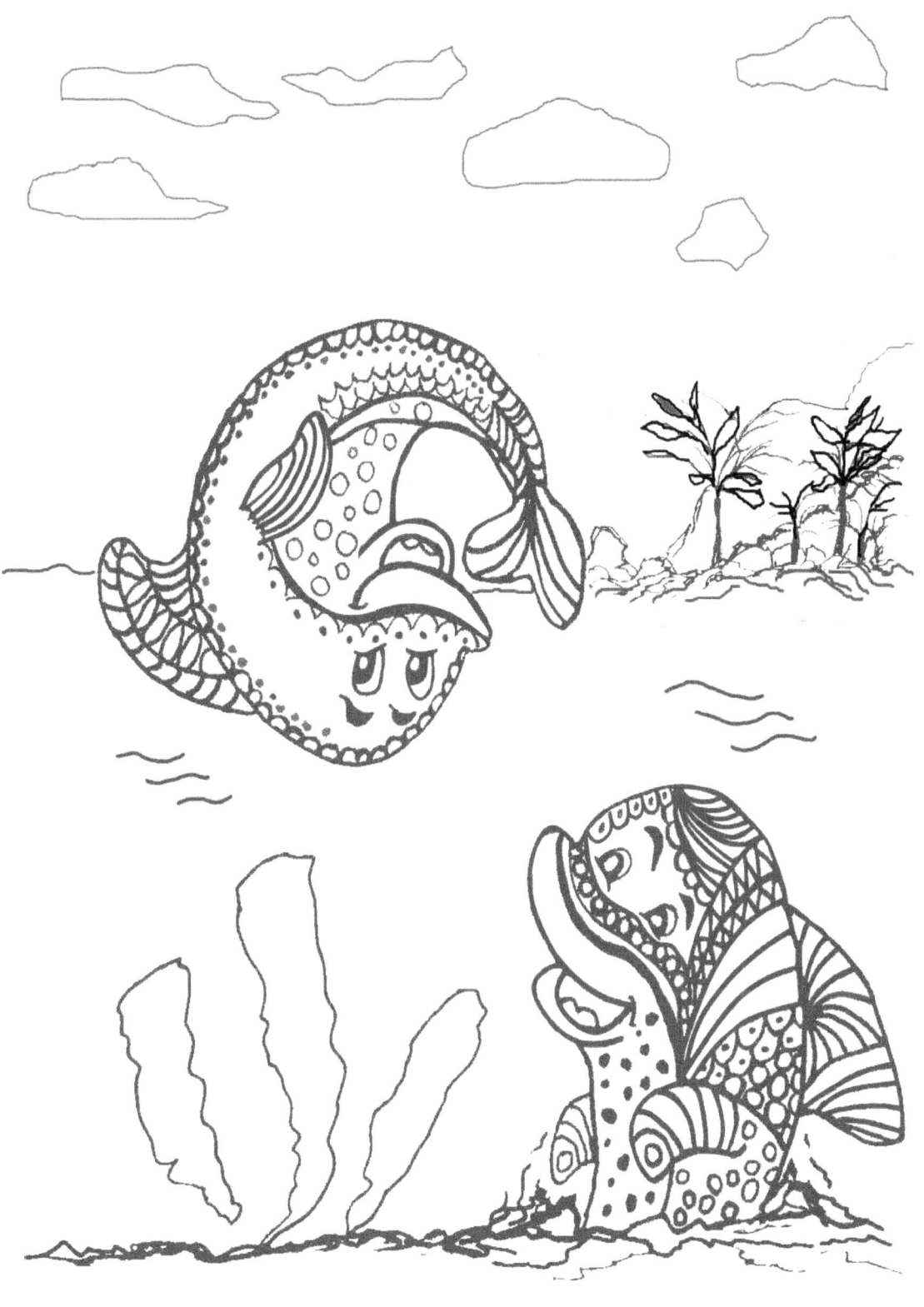

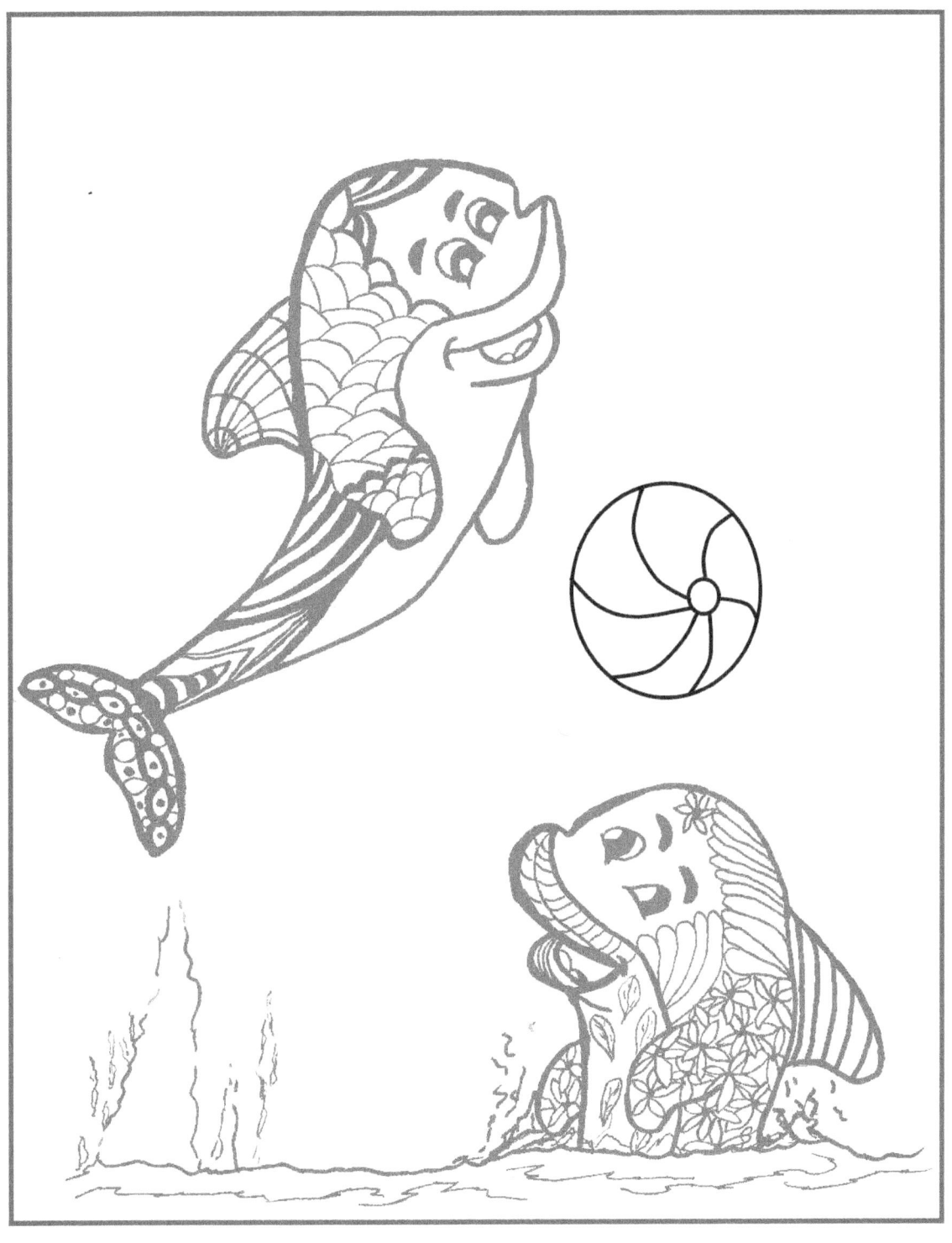

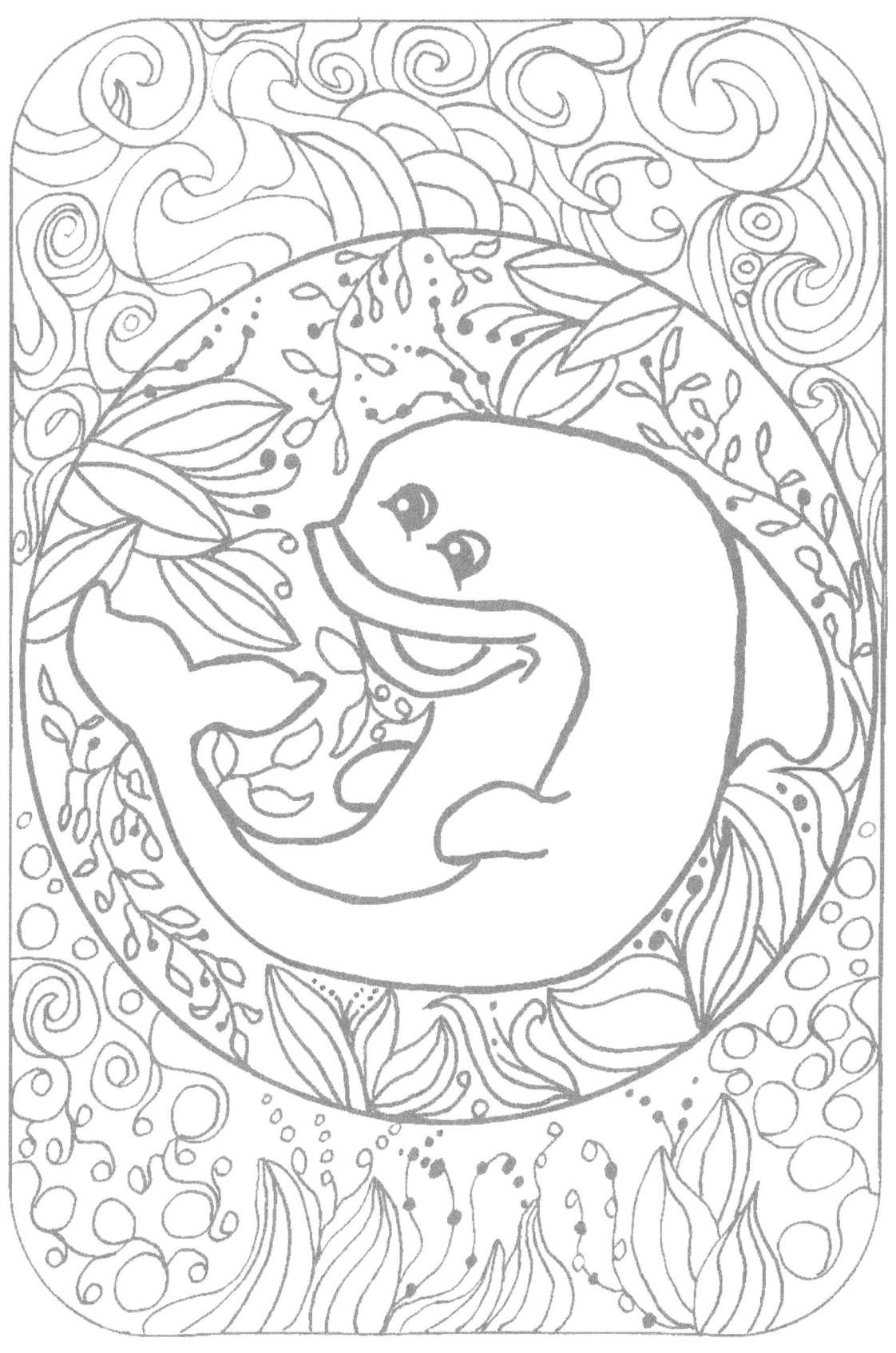

Kaye Dennan

Magic Number   14

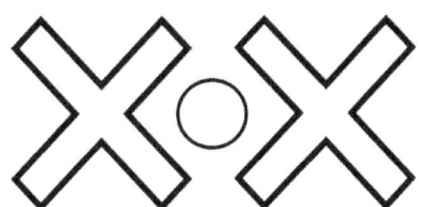

1. Write it   _____

2. Draw it   _____

3. Add 3   _____

4. Subtract 6   _____

5. Add 5   _____

6. Subtract 3   _____

7. Next 3 numbers ____ ____ ____

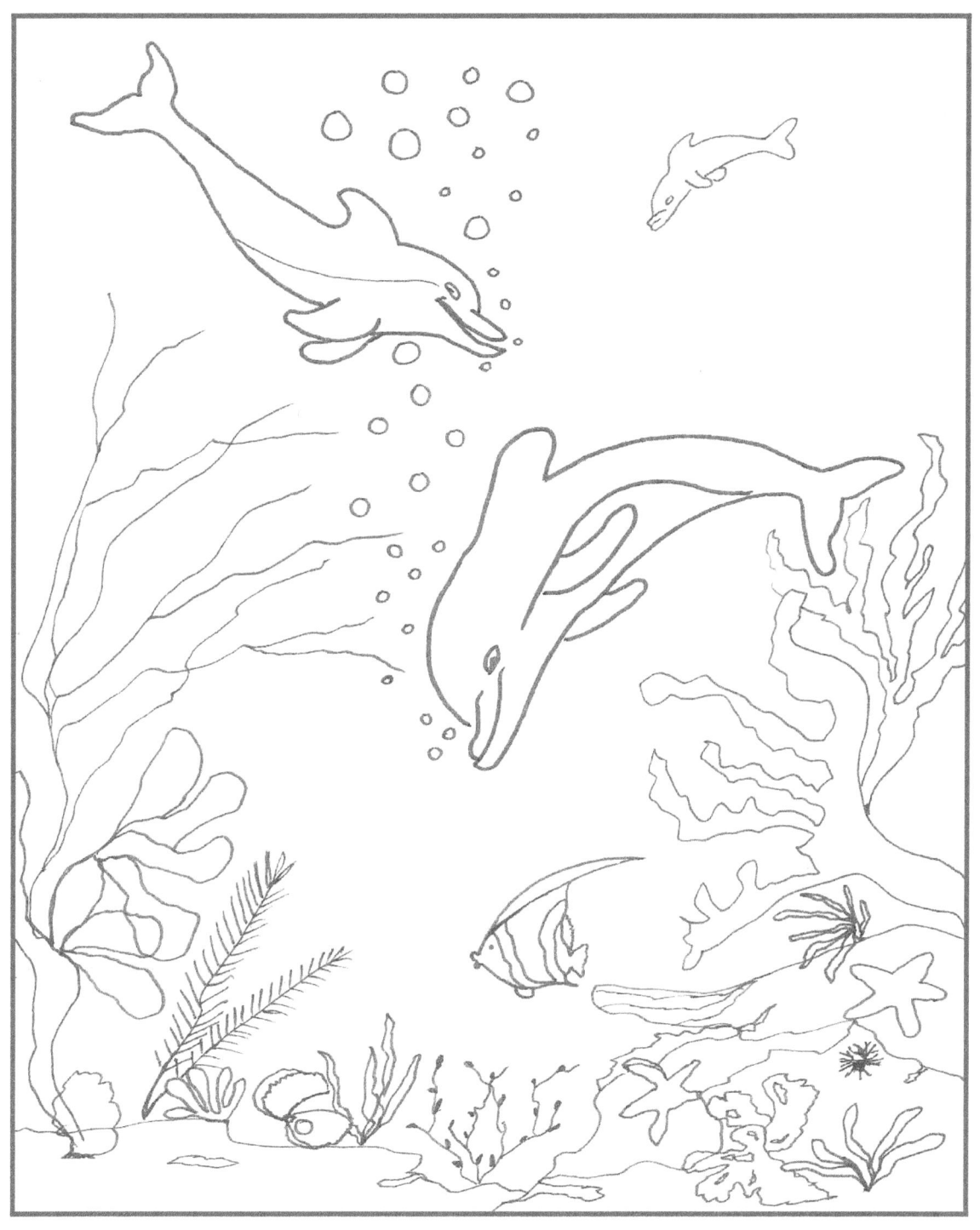

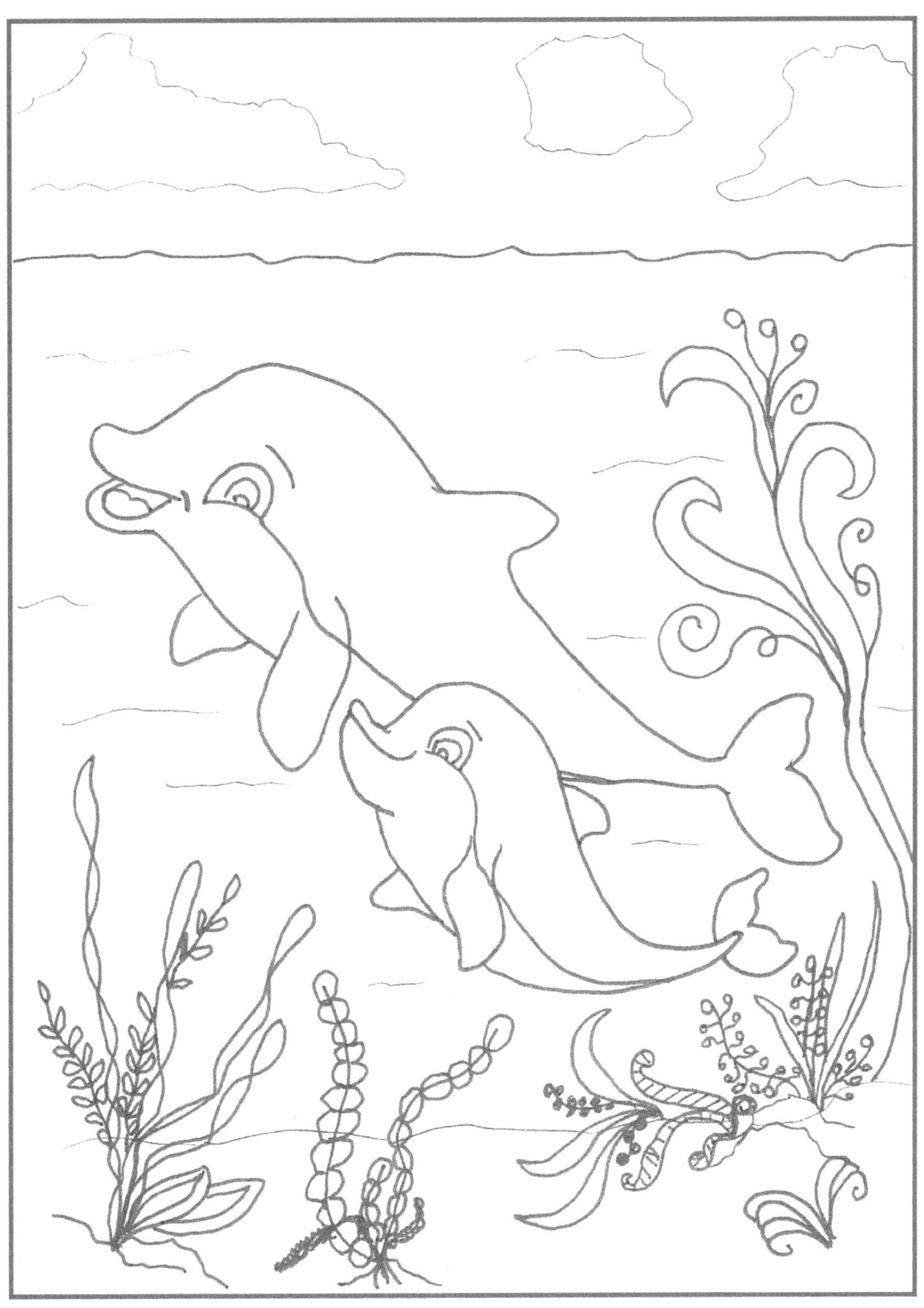

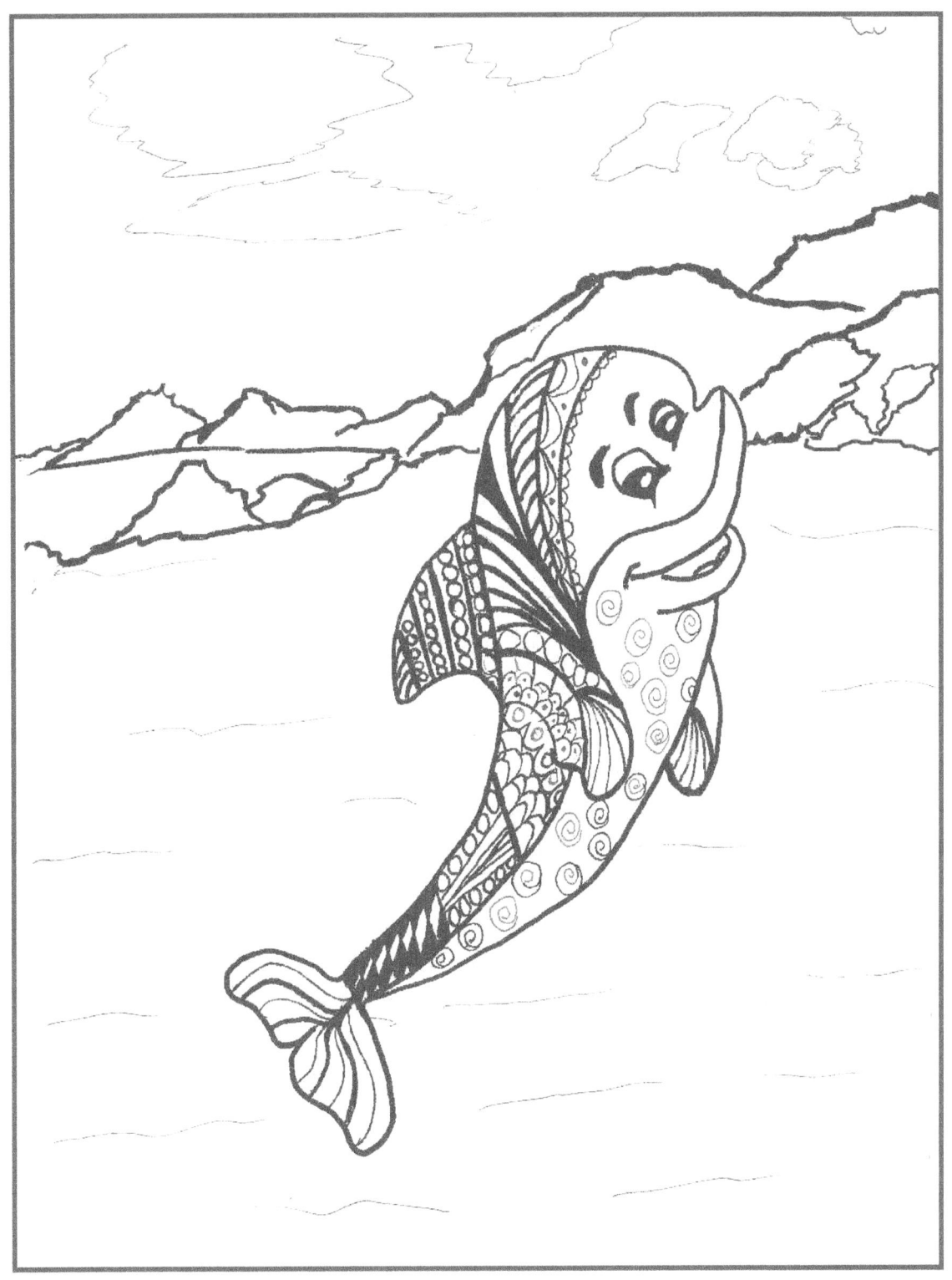

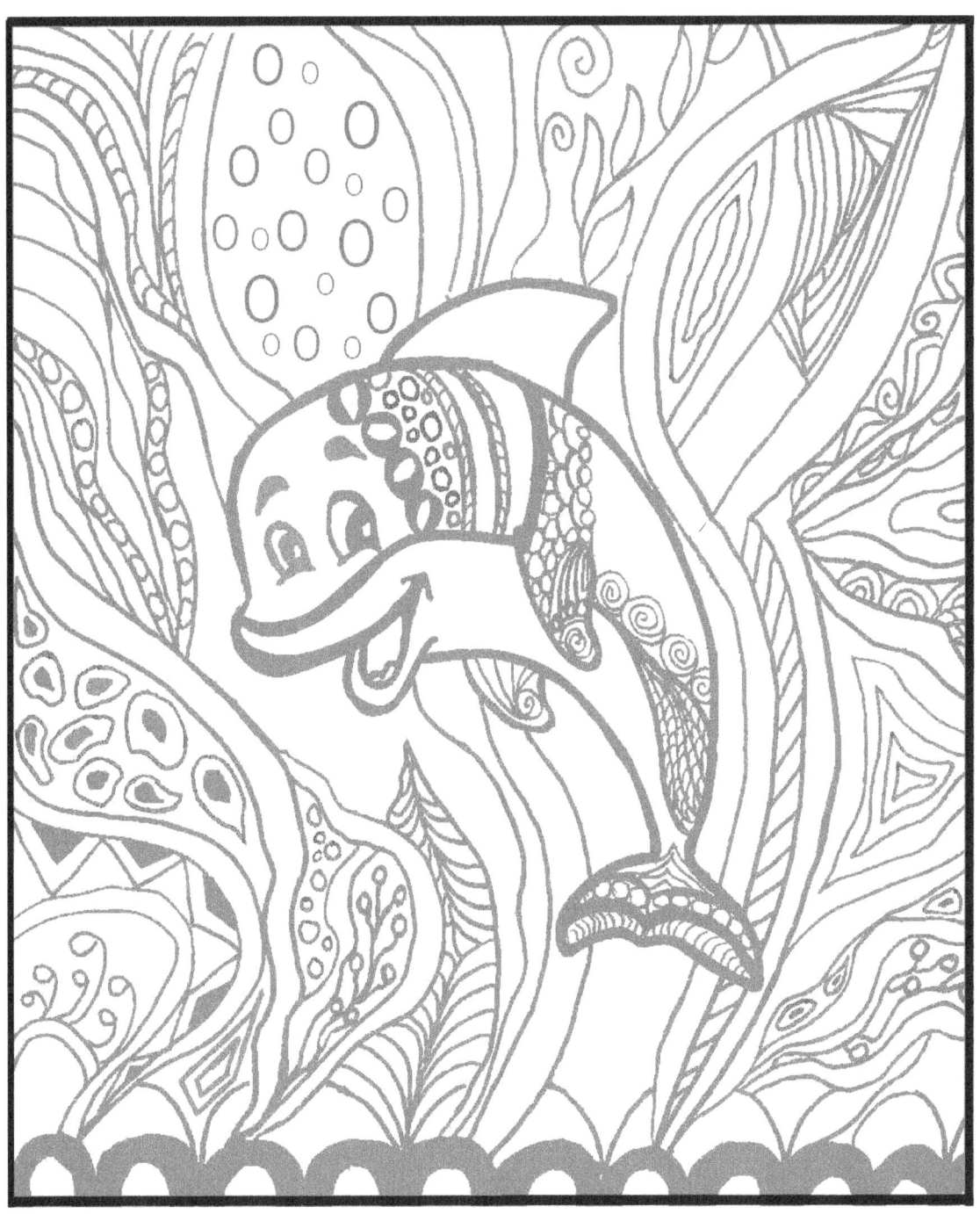

Magic Number 11

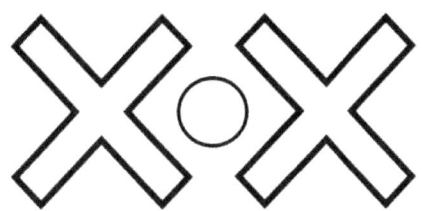

1. Write it _____

2. Draw it _____

3. Add 4 _____

4. Subtract 5 _____

5. Add 6 _____

6. Subtract 4 _____

7. Next 3 numbers ____ ____ ____

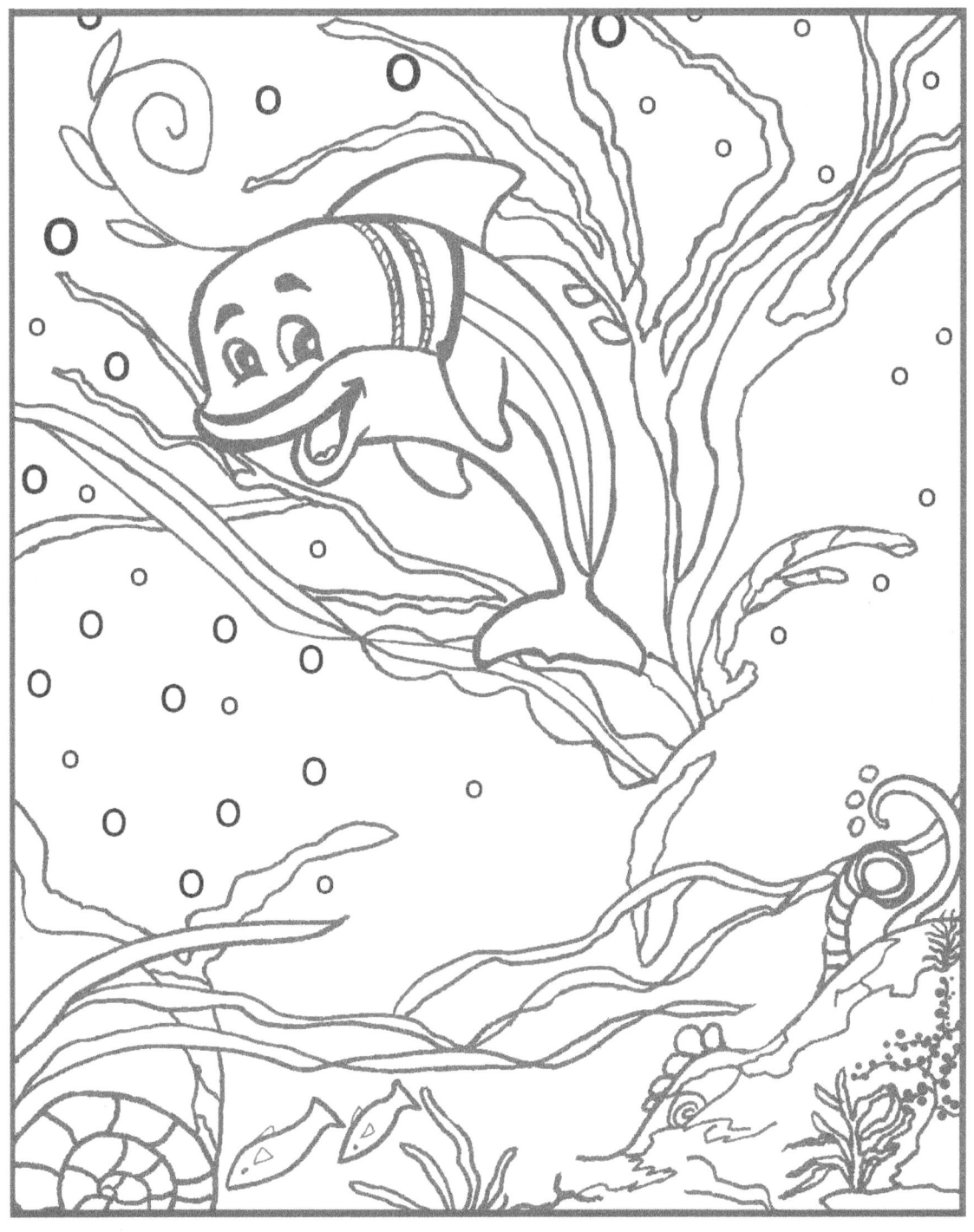

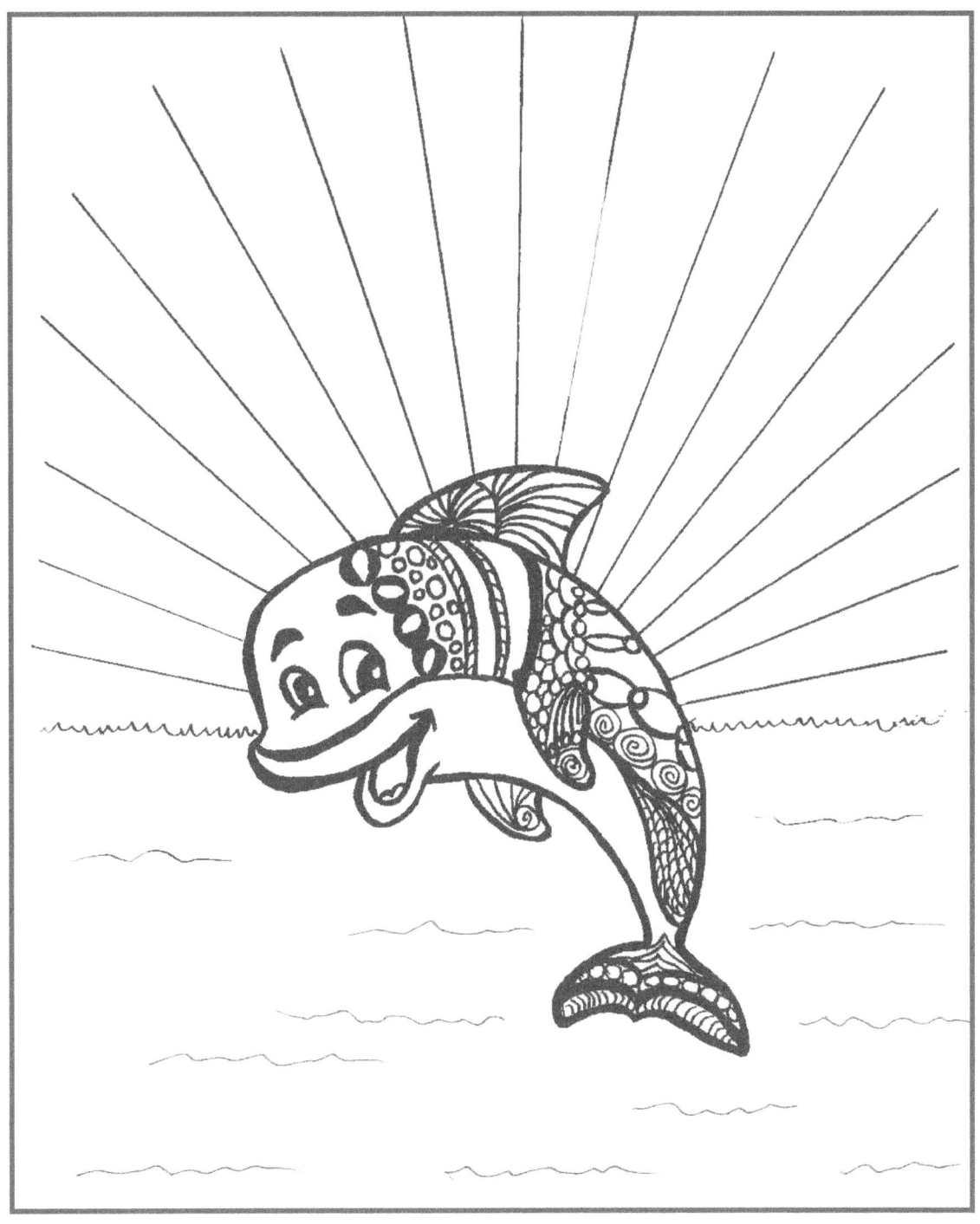

Dolphins are a favorite of mine and I hope you have enjoyed this coloring book.

More paperback coloring books can be sourced through

KD COLORING STUDIO
http://www.kdcoloring.com

Coloring and activity books for children can be purchased by searching for my author name:

Kaye Dennan

https://www.createspace.com/